Table of Contents

Introduction

We see it everyday, everywhere we look. It's on the television in everything we watch, even down to the commercials. The tender touches and deep longing stares. If it could have a visual effect it would be sparks. That's intimacy. It's that deeper connection that we all want to experience. I get tons of letters from readers with relationship problems that are seeking advice. More often than not, the problem is that someone has lost that loving feeling and the question is how to get it back ?

It is normal and natural to desire more from your relationship. The intimate connection that you have with your partner is what sustains you when the going gets a little difficult. It makes you love harder and longer. Sometimes as we go through life, physical displays of affection are not always possible with our partners. These intimate types of bonds are so necessary because they can be as fulfilling, if not more so than any other.

Intimacy is not some mythical existence that only the few can have. It's the balancing factor for any and every successful relationship. Once you have a better understanding of what it is, you will have an easier time reaching your goals. Combining knowledge and experience, this book will help you to remove the obstacles that we all have encountered, thus assisting you to create and improve your current relationship. You too can have the sparks in your relationship that we all desire.

WHAT IS INTIMACY

Intimacy is defined as a close association or deep loving relationship with another person. Intimacy is a feeling of familiarity, a deep knowledge of another person. Intimacy is one of the basic elements in the hierarchy of existence. It is necessary for emotional well being and it is not something that appears overnight. The intimate connection is one that develops over time, with nurturing and close interaction with another.

It is something that exists in all animals, wild or tame. It is evident in the way primates tenderly groom and caress each other. It is evident in the way birds and reptiles perform there instinctual rituals when they are trying to attract and entice the opposite sex. You don't have to be able to speak to show those feelings, that type of closeness comes from an intimate bond.

It's a feeling and a very intense and satisfying one. When done correctly, it is the ultimate form of non- verbal communication. It can be the most fulfilling part of a relationship and we all want it, crave it and desire it. Developing the intimate side of your relationship can elevate it and intensify your level of desire for one another. Nurturing the intimate side of your relationship is a necessary step to achieve balance and harmony. It's the key to longevity and a lifetime of bliss.

Intimacy vs Sex

If you could, assemble 100 people of various stages of adulthood, walks of life and races and ask them this question. Is there a difference between intimacy and sex? If you had a choice between having one or the other in a relationship, which would you choose? You would be surprised to know that the vast majority would choose, that's right, intimacy.

Intimacy is a feeling. It can be sensual or spiritual and it is created by a deep and close bond. Sex is merely a physical act. Sex is a physical instinct, so to speak. It is necessary to procreate, for the continuation of existence. Any successful relationship needs both to survive and grow. When it comes down to it, intimacy equals longevity and is the winner, hands down.

Now, let's take a stroll down memory lane. I want you to think about your most satisfying and intense sexual relationship. What made that person a champion, so to speak? Aside from athleticism and stamina, the two of you probably had an intense connection.

Some people know how to push all the right buttons, at all the right times. They have intimacy down to a science and they have perfectly customized it to there advantage. Not an easy task, but it is definitely one that we all can accomplish and conquer.

Barriers

So how is it that we know what intimacy is? After we know
what it is, how do we get it? How do we get to that deeper level
of intimacy? For many of us, there are many roadblocks on the
path to intimacy. The most common barrier is communication,
the most elusive one is time. Sometimes, it's just that we are to
shy to speak up about what we want from our partners.

Did you ever get the feeling that you were talking and your mate
wasn't listening? Of course you have and you are not alone. It is
very hard to discuss important topics if no one is paying
attention. It could be that your timing is off. It's all about
timing. After working hard all day, no one wants to hear about
any issues the minute they walk in the door. Save that for
another time, perhaps in the morning when your brain is actually
on full powered and you are more clear headed. You know when
your mate is most attentive and that's when you should discuss

important things. Don't wait until the last minute when it's a full on crisis approaching. Timing is everything and a critical key for successful communication.

When it starts to feel like your partner is losing focus and zoning out, abort the conversation and restart it at a later time. Learning when to talk about things makes for better communication between the two of you. Timing your conversations is one of the most important keys to successful communication.

With today's economy, two incomes, sometimes three are often needed to make ends meet. With childcare being so expensive these days, many couples opt to work opposite shifts in order to cut down on the childcare expenses. This can make you and your partner feel like two ships passing in the night. So when do you see each other?

When you and your partner work opposite hours, communication isn't always easy. So what's the solution? The easiest solution is to compromise. Somebody may have to sacrifice a few hours of sleep so that the two of you can communicate. Everyone needs there sleep, so don't hesitate to take a nap. Set an alarm to wake you up at a time when the two of you can talk.

Even while you are at work, you can make your break time, mate time. Take a few minutes during your break to call your partner just to say hello. Tell them you love them or how much you appreciate them.

Handwritten sentiments are a beautiful way to show someone that you care. Write a note or a letter and leave it on your partner's pillow. If they carry a briefcase, tuck it inside so that they can be delightfully surprised when they open it. If you don't know what to say, buy a card and scribble a little note inside. You can always spray it with your favorite scent and mail it to them at work or home. It will give them something to think about and it gives the two of you something to talk about.

Another good way of communication is text and instant messaging. It's not just for kids anymore. Many of the newer cell phones now have voice and video recording capabilities. They all have cameras so you can send pictures and love notes all day to your partner if you choose. You can also send your mate a steamy voice note or a cute 30 second video right to their cell phone, it's a great way to stay in touch and keep you on your other half's mind.

Relationship Evaluation

This exercise can be done individually or as a couple. Every relationship has its good points and bad points, so first things first. The purpose of this exercise is to put your life with your partner on paper. It will help you to assess your relationship as a whole. A lot of times, it is not as gloomy as you may think. You just need to see it for yourself and identify areas that you may want to make better. It will give you a starting point. It's also a good idea to keep a journal so that you can track your journey as a couple.

Items Needed

piece of paper, preferably a journal

pen

open mind

Draw a line down the sheet of paper

Write all the things that you would like to do differently on the left side- (We will refer to them as soon to be positive, not negative)

Write positive on the right- (We will refer to them as positively perfect)

List all the things about your relationship that you would like to improve on.

This can be time you spend, things you like to do as a couple, etc. This can also be the things that you just want to make better or do differently. On the opposite side of the paper, write all the things that you like about your relationship.

Relationship Affirmation

After you have taken the time to think of all the things that you want to improve in your relationship, take your time and sort things out in your mind. After you have identified the areas that you want to improve, you need to make a daily reminder for yourself. Write it out on a sheet of pretty paper or print it out on your computer. However you do it, it needs to be done and placed where you can see it on a daily basis. Let it be a reminder on what your goals are and use it as a tool to keep you focused on the task at hand. Visualization is one of the many ways to achieve a goal, if you can see it, you will believe it and then you can and will do it. When writing your affirmation, always write it as if it is happening now.

Do not use negative words or phrases in your affirmation, keep the energy positive at all times. Read it at the start and end of your day, every day. You will start to see a difference in your relationship and have the energy to continue with the process.

Communication Techniques

This is designed to help you be a more effective communicator. Effective communication starts with effective listening. Here are some tips to help you to become a more effective communicator with your partner. Try them out with your partner, practice makes perfect.

Non verbal tips

Lean in and listen – leaning in closer to the other person shows that you are interested in what they are saying to you. It also helps you to focus on what is being said during the course of the conversation.

Make eye contact- it helps to establish and maintain an open line of communication during the conversation

Touch- touching is very therapeutic. If the conversation warrants physical contact, reach out and touch.

Verbal communication tips

Repeat the facts- it shows the person that you are paying attention.

Think before you speak – this will ensure that you are saying exactly what you need to say.

Take a deep breath – it helps you to relax and it also will help you to maintain calm if the conversation is starting to escalate into an unpleasant experience.

Don't interrupt- allow the other person a chance to get there point across without interrupting their thought process. It is frustrating and it makes the other person feel as if their concerns are irrelevant.

It Starts With You

Now that we have established ways to improve your communication and more effective ways to get your point across, it's time to turn the focus to the most important person, yourself. It all starts with you and the most important thing is to make time for yourself. If you have children, like many of us that can often be easier said than done.

You have to take a little time for yourself to recharge your batteries. It's extremely difficult to make time for your partner if you don't have time for yourself. Planning ahead is necessary to stay one step ahead of the game and is the easiest way to squeeze more hours in to your day.

One simple tip is to plan your meals and prepare for the next day, the night before. Make ahead and pre-prepped meals are a time and a lifesaver. Cook it once, eat it twice. Many dishes freeze well and can be used at a later date, even as another dish. With a little planning and a lot of practice, it gets easier.

It is near impossible to take care of everyone else if you are neglecting your own needs. We all need a moment to breath and recharge and I can't stress that enough. Spend some time doing activities that interest you as often as you can. Start saving those pennies and treat yourself to a day of pampering on a regular basis. Pampering is what ever you define it as, be it a housekeeper to come in monthly or a night on the town with your friends. With a little planning and a lot of practice, it gets easier.

If you resolved to get healthier, do it. Start small and do your research. Speak with your doctor before starting any exercise or diet regimen. You don't want to do anything to yourself that is harmful. Build healthy habits by doing a little bit everyday. Start with something that you can handle, it just takes 30 days for something to become a habit. I always recommend taking a multi-vitamin daily and making sure you drink adequate amounts of water everyday. Your body needs energy to move and water keeps your body functioning at peak performance. Exercise is important to maintain healthy joint movement and flexibility. So do your research, pick a healthy regimen for yourself and get to it.

Lastly, seek balance. This means all the aspects of your life. Relationships are the most important, no matter who you are. We all have relationships with our families, our friends and our partners. For things to go smooth, it takes balance. So if you have children, spend more time with them. Family bonds are just as important as any other. Make a date night with your kids and let them pick the activity. If you have a circle of friends, spend time with them too. Your bonds with your family and friends are what helped to make you into the wonderful person that you are. So nurture those bonds and spend a little time with all the people that bring you joy.

Sensuality

It's hard to discuss intimacy without its counterpart sensuality. Sensuality involves stimulating the senses. It's that feel good feeling that we find so addicting, its excitement. Once you conquer the barriers to one, you magically unlock the door to the other. It should be a total body concept, when thinking of ways to improve your relationship. Always focus on using and stimulating all of your senses.

You walk in to a room and all eyes are on you. Mouths agape, jaws drop when you pass. Strangers glaring, wanting and waiting for the opportunity to say," Hello, would you happen to have the time?"

That killer confidence, that certain something that makes you the center of attention. Some call it, "je ne sais quoi"; others may call it "sex appeal". Whatever you may call it, you had it and at some point it vanished, like a thief in the night. There was a time when your mate couldn't keep their eyes or hands off of you, now they seem to be moving away. Well you have to get it back and I'm here to tell you how.

Gentleman, let's start with you first. Think back to your first date, how you went to the barber to get a fresh cut. How you made sure your clothes fit just right and wrinkle free. You smelled, oh so sexy and looked, so fresh and so clean, right? Well that's how you attracted your mate. So you have to use what you had to get what you want. So first things first, just how you like when you like the way you look with a fresh cut, ladies love it too. Nothing says sexy like a well groomed man.

Now, go through that wardrobe and take a good look at what you have. Sometimes it's just a matter of matching things up a little differently to get a new outlook on your attire. Back away from the oversized tees please! Men wear collars and a shirt with a collar can go a long way. It can dress up a nice pair of jeans or add a sweater and a nice jacket for a night on the town.

Just remember, it's all about the buttons. Take a look at magazines and what the men your age are wearing on television if you need a suggestion. Mannequins in the store are always dressed in the current fashion and you can take notes from the sales people in the stores as well.

So now that you look good, how do you smell? Humans are scent attracted by nature and your mate is no different. We truly appreciate a good smelling man; but don't overdo it! Back away from the heavy colognes and try fragrance oils. They absorb nicely into the skin and mixed with body lotion after a shower, make you irresistible from head to toe. The scent will last a long time and it won't overpower the room when you enter or leave.

This is the start of a new journey for you and while we often think of what to change, we neglect the easiest thing to change. How we smell. As I mentioned before in my article, people are scent attracted. It's a fact of nature and it's one of the easiest things to change. So if you are not sure where to begin or what to do next, here is a quick breakdown for the ladies.

Women's Scents Can be Broken Down into 4 Main Categories:

Floral- anything to do with flowers. These scents are very feminine and romantic and can be worn in the day or evening. *Gardenia, lilac, lavender, etc.*

Woody-these scents are spicy and earthy. They are more exotic and sensual and are better for evening. *Patchouli, cinnamon, sandalwood and amber.*

Fresh- Clean and natural scents. These are clean and playful and are good for the day or evening as well. They are often blended with herbal scents or water based scents.

These include *orange, grapefruit mandarin orange, etc*

Oriental –These are the heavy hitters. These are the most sensual fragrances that men adore. They are commonly blended with spice scents or exotic flowers and are best worn in the evening. These are the *vanillas, sugars, chocolates, etc.*

Now the best way to decide which scent works on you, apply it lightly and allow it to air dry for at least 15 minutes. Walk around the store a while and allow the scent to mingle with your own natural scent. Secondly consider the occasion for which you will be wearing the fragrance. If you want to drive your partner wild, pick from the wood or oriental family. If you want a clean smell for daytime and everyday, pick from the fresh category.

It is best to go to a store where they have full size testers where you can apply it and let it dissipate. The most important rule is, wear what works well with you. Don't apply to much and layer for a longer lasting fragrance. Try a shower gel, a body lotion and a body mist of all the same scent for a longer lasting fragrance. So take a shopping spree and discover your scent of attraction.

Men's fragrances are a little more complicated and have more classifications. It is best to let your partner choose his or her own fragrance. If you are purchasing it as a gift, pay attention and take note of what they wear now. If he or she has a scent that smells good on them, take the name to the fragrance counter and ask for help. Choosing something in the same category is a sure fire way to pick out a scent that works well with his or her body chemistry.

Going shopping for a new fragrance can be a fun experience and it is a great idea to take your partner with you. The two of you can try out different scents and you can see the effect they have on your partner. Make a day of it and enjoy that time alone with your mate.

Setting the Mood with the 5 Senses

Take a look at your shared space. Your space is your sanctuary and we all like what is pleasing to the eye. Your area should be clean and appealing to all the senses. You should always make sure that before you go forward with things, you are looking your best and you are most importantly relaxed and comfortable.

Nobody wants to be in the same space as someone that they don't find visually appealing. So take that into consideration first and foremost and take the time to pull your self together. Next is lighting, you should use a dimmer switch or candle light to soften the overall ambiance in the room.

Smell

I'm a big fan of aromatherapy. Aromatherapy is based on the effect that natural fragrances have on the body and mind. Fragrances have an influence what we think and how we feel when we smell them.

Essential oils are best for this and I recommend using them to enhance the smell of your area. Try using them with a heat source to help them permeate the air. This can be done with incense, oil burners diffusers or candles. If you don't have any of the above you can always place a few drops in to a pot of simmering water and allow the scent to fragrance the room.

Being that essential oils are very concentrated and can harm the skin if used incorrectly, I suggest that you always use them in the above manner.

Many oils have several uses and some can be blended together for a combined effect. For the purpose of this project we will focus on a small selection. Always use trial and error when blending oils and with a little practice, you will be able to make the perfect scent for your personal uses.

Stress Relief - Bergamot

Cedarwood

Chamomile

Lavender

Marjoram

Jasmine

Energy-   Peppermint

           Lemon

           Rosemary

           Grapefruit

           Eucalyptus

           Ginger

Aphrodisiac – Patchouli

                Sandalwood

                Cinnamon

                Clove

                Vanilla

                Ylang Ylang

Jasmine

Rose

Sounds

Always remove all possible noise distractions from your area. If
you choose to play music, it should be low and soothing.
Soothing is whatever you interpret it to be and you should play
what appeals to you. Instrumental music is the best or light and
smooth jazz. If the music is instrumental, your partner can easily
focus on you, not the song lyrics. Natural sounds are great too
and can help relax and soothe you and your mate after a long
day. Gentle rainfall, ocean sounds whatever you find soothing.
It's about what affects you and puts you at ease.

Taste

Feeding each other finger foods can be a very intimate experience. You can prepare a meal together or order something to go. Desserts and fruit are excellent choices and can be a very sensual experience when being fed to you by another person. To spice things up, try using a blindfold. Cover your partner's eyes with a satin or silk scarf. Tell them that no hands are allowed and feed them items one at a time. They have to guess what it is, you can give them a few seconds to guess. The reward for winning or losing is up to you.

Touch

We all love to be touched and the skin is the largest organ in the body. Massages are great and we all like them, but try a twist on it. As I mentioned before, blindfolds are excellent. When you are unable to see, all the other senses are heightened. So you are more sensitive to touch. Try using different objects to massage and stimulate your partner. Feathers, massagers and warming packs make excellent starters.

Try varying the amount of pressure and placement of the different objects. Always take into account what your partner likes and dislikes. The feet are very sensitive and full of pressure points. Men like foot massages just as much as women. You can draw a foot bath for your partner and let them soak their feet in some scented bath salts. Rub and massage them while they are soaking, take note of what feels good to your mate.

The options are endless and you can make it a very pleasurable experience if you use all of the senses to stimulate each other. Keep an open mind and remember that this is a learning experience and above all, it should be pleasurable to both of you.

INTIMACY ENHANCING TECHNIQUES

PLEASURE BOX

Items needed

Pretty box with a hat or similar type container

Pretty paper or note cards - blank

Pen

Your partner

Give your partner half of the note cards or paper and you keep the other half. Think of some of the different sensual and intimate activities that you liked sharing or would like to try. If it is something that you haven't tried before, explain it in the back of the note card or paper. After you are done, fold them in half and place them in the box. Now comes the fun part, whenever you feel the need or urge to spice things up, take out the box and leave it on the bed. When your partner finds the box they have to pick a card from the box. That will be the chosen activity for the evening.

This activity is a good one because it involves communication and imagination. It will be a reminder of all the fun you had coming up with the activities. It also involves spending quality time with each other. It will take time and imagination to fill out the cards and it will give you an idea of how much alone time you need to set aside for each other for the chosen activity.

HEART TO HEART

Items needed

Candle light or a dim room

Quiet area

Your partner

Get yourselves in to a comfortable position, on the bed or the floor. You and your partner need to be face to face and able to touch one another. Now, place your hand on your partner's chest, over there heart. Allow them to do the same to you. Now close your eyes and focus on the rhythm of each others heart beating. Take some deep slow breaths and feel how your partners rhythm changes. The sound of the heart beating is very comforting and soothing. Look into your partners eyes, look at their face. Tell them how you feel about them. Notice how their heartbeat changes. Hold the position as long as you are comfortable. Spend the time together and use it as a little escape from the everyday.

Nature Retreat

Items needed

Sleeping bag for 2

Picnic basket and cooler

Finger foods and the like

Candles and lanterns

Invitation

Give your partner an invitation for a nature retreat, either mail it or leave it on the pillow. Make it a nice one but don't say where you are going, make it a surprise. There is no need to pack clothes because you are going to do it at home indoors. Clear a space in your living room or den and set up a mock camp. Bring some elements from outdoors inside, pretty leaves, pinecones, use your imagination.

 Set up camp and surround the area with candles and use the lantern as a campfire. The two of you will only have each other and you can use this time to do whatever tickles your fancy. When its time for bed, unroll your sleeping bag for two and cuddle up.

Words from the Author

The intimacy project is a vehicle to start you on your journey to a more satisfying relationship. It is a key to unlock your mind and allow you to explore. There is no right or wrong way to interpret this project. There is no pass or fail. The project is ongoing and is just one step in a series to help couples achieve that balance that they all need. Life is to complicated and we so often get all tied up in the day to day that we forget what makes us happy. I hope that you enjoyed the first step of your journey to a closer bond and a more nurturing and satisfying relationship. I look forward to helping you create many lasting memories with your partner.

Peace and Blessings

A Relationship Defined

A Poem by DaDiva

Time....

has a rhythm all its own.

Like the moon, how it seduces the vast expanse of oceans,

creating it's familiar ebb and flow.

Lust.....

powerful emotions from deep within,

causing excitement, burning, tingling, pulsations.

Passion.......

exploding eruptions, stealing breath before it escapes.

ecstasy, unwilling to submit to control.

Make time.....

for each other.

For stolen moments and whispered promises.

Look into their eyes, that's where lust resides.

Make them remember the passion.

Your sensual undulations that are unmatched by no other,

ever.

Relationships....

are all of these things and so much more.

Intensity of these three elements, determine your fate.

Be truthful always, even when it hurts.

www.ingramcontent.com/pod-product-compliance
Lightning Source LLC
Chambersburg PA
CBHW050350290526
45785CB00006B/2707